Dear Parent:

Congratulations! Your child is taking the first steps on an exciting journey. The destination? Independent reading!

STEP INTO READING® will help your child get there. The program five steps to reading success. Each step includes fun stories and color There are also Step into Reading Sticker Books, Step into Reading M Readers, Step into Reading Write-In Readers, Step into Reading Phonics Readers, and Step into Reading Phonics First Steps! Boxed Sets—a complete literacy program with something for every child.

Learning to Read, Step by Step!

Ready to Read   Preschool–Kindergarten
• big type and easy words • rhyme and rhythm • picture clues
For children who know the alphabet and are eager to begin reading.

Reading with Help   Preschool–Grade 1
• basic vocabulary • short sentences • simple stories
For children who recognize familiar words and sound out new words with help.

Reading on Your Own   Grades 1–3
• engaging characters • easy-to-follow plots • popular topics
For children who are ready to read on their own.

Reading Paragraphs   Grades 2–3
• challenging vocabulary • short paragraphs • exciting stories
For newly independent readers who read simple sentences with confidence.

Ready for Chapters   Grades 2–4
• chapters • longer paragraphs • full-color art
For children who want to take the plunge into chapter books but still like colorful pictures.

STEP INTO READING® is designed to give every child a successful reading experience. The grade levels are only guides. Children can progress through the steps at their own speed, developing confidence in their reading, no matter what their grade.

Remember, a lifetime love of reading starts with a single step!

To Daniel Penner

Thanks to Dr. David Grimaldi
of the American Museum of Natural History
for his helpful advice.

Text copyright © 1996 by Lucille Recht Penner. Illustrations copyright © 1996 by Pamela Johnson. All rights reserved under International and Pan-American Copyright Conventions. Published in the United States by Random House Children's Books, a division of Random House, Inc., New York, and simultaneously in Canada by Random House of Canada Limited, Toronto.

www.stepintoreading.com

Educators and librarians, for a variety of teaching tools, visit us at www.randomhouse.com/teachers

Library of Congress Cataloging-in-Publication Data
Penner, Lucille Recht.
Monster bugs / by Lucille Recht Penner ; illustrated by Pamela Johnson.
    p.   cm. — (Step into reading. A step 3 book)   Originally published: New York : Random House, 1996, in series: Step into reading. Step 2 book.
SUMMARY: Describes some of the world's largest insects and spiders, including the Goliath beetle, praying mantis, tarantula, and giant atlas moth.
ISBN 0-679-86974-3 (trade) — ISBN 0-679-96974-8 (lib. bdg.)
1. Insects—Juvenile literature.   2. Insects—Size—Juvenile literature.   3. Spiders—Juvenile literature.   4. Spiders—Size—Juvenile literature.   [1. Insects.   2. Spiders.]   I. Johnson, Pamela, ill.   II. Title.   III. Series: Step into reading. Step 3 book.
QL467.2.P458   2003   595.7—dc21   2002013442

Printed in the United States of America   23 22 21 20 19 18

STEP INTO READING, RANDOM HOUSE, and the Random House colophon are registered trademarks of Random House, Inc.

STEP INTO READING®

STEP 3

Monster Bugs

by Lucille Recht Penner

illustrated by Pamela Johnson

Random House 🏠 New York

Have you ever
looked at a bug
<u>up close</u>?
You might see horns
or armor or spikes.
If bugs were your size,
they'd be scary.

No bug is as big as you.
But some are huge for bugs.
And some are fierce!
This book is all about
the biggest and fiercest bugs
in the world.

The heaviest bug
is the goliath beetle of Africa.
How heavy is it?
Get two eggs
out of the fridge.
Hold them together
in your hand.
That's how heavy
<u>one</u> goliath beetle is.

But goliath beetles
are gentle.
Some kids even keep them
as pets!

Not all beetles
are gentle.
The giant stag beetle
is a fighter!

These two beetles
are fighting over
a female.

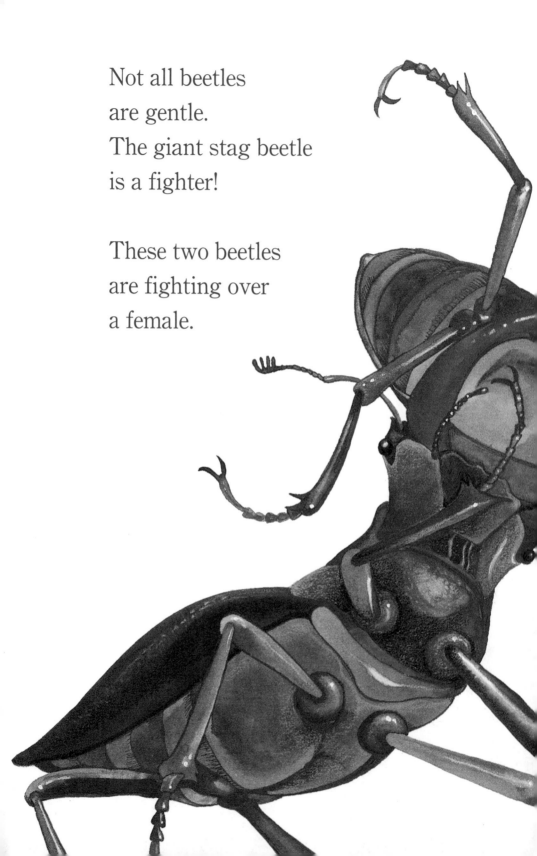

One male grabs the other
in its huge jaws,
lifts it into the air,
and slams it down
on the ground!

A mouse wants to eat
this juicy bombardier beetle.
But the beetle
fires boiling-hot gas
from its rear end.

Bang! Bang! Bang!
Each burst explodes
like a firecracker.
The gas bombs
burn and sting,
and the mouse
runs away.

Giant waterbugs
stab their victims
and suck their blood
like vampires!

The mother waterbug
glues her eggs
to the father's back.
He carries them around
until they hatch.
Then, if the babies don't
swim away quickly,
he might eat them!

What's the stinkiest,
smelliest bug?
A stinkbug.

When a bird
scares a stinkbug,
the bug oozes
a horrible, smelly
liquid.

The bird flies away.
It doesn't want
a dinner
that stinks.

Australian
walking sticks
are the longest
of all bugs.
Hungry birds
love to eat them.

The walking stick
doesn't have big jaws
or burning gas
to fight with.
But it can
hold very still
and hide.
Look closely.
Can you see it
against this branch?

Some praying mantises
are as long as bananas.

This one jabs
a curious frog
with the spikes on its legs.
Pow! Pow!
The frog hops away.

A praying mantis
will eat anything
smaller than itself.
Even a baby bird
that falls from its nest.
After eating, the mantis
washes its face
like a kitten.

Army ants are killers.
Millions of them
march through the forest.

They eat anything
they can catch—
cockroaches, spiders, beetles,
and scorpions.

When they come
to a village,
even people hurry
to get out
of their way.

<u>Grrrrrrr!</u>
Imagine falling into
a lion's den.
It's happening
to these ants.
A hungry ant lion
has dug a pit.
It hides at the bottom,
buried in sand.
Only its powerful
jaws stick out.

When an ant falls in,
the ant lion grabs it,
sucks it dry,
and throws away the shell.

The body of a female
black widow spider
is smaller than a dime,
but her poison
is stronger
than a rattlesnake's.

How did the
black widow
get its name?
Sometimes the female
spider kills and eats
her mate!

The raft spider
eats tadpoles
and little fish.

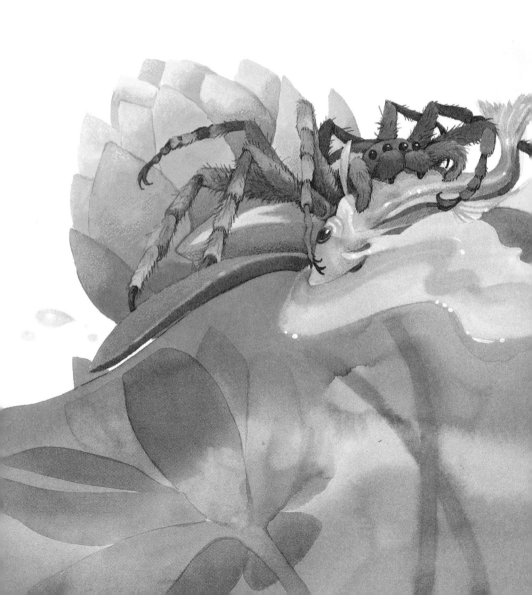

It stabs a minnow
with its deadly fangs,
pulls it
out of the water,
and gobbles it up.

Tarantulas are hairy spiders.
A big one would cover
your dinner plate.

Most tarantulas are gentle.
But some have
an unusual weapon—
their own hair.

When a coyote
tries to eat it,
the tarantula kicks
a cloud of itchy hairs
into the air.
The hairs make the coyote
cough and scratch.
Now the tarantula
can escape.

A tarantula's worst enemy
is a fierce wasp called
a tarantula hawk.

The spider tries to
fight off the wasp.
But the wasp darts in
and stings it.

Now the spider can't move.
The wasp drags it into its burrow
and lays an egg on it.
After the egg hatches,
the baby wasp
eats the tarantula alive.

Have you ever been
stung by a bee?
It hurts!

One bee sting
is bad enough.
But how about
hundreds of stings?
Killer bees are
smaller than other bees—
but a lot fiercer.
When they get mad,
they chase and sting
their enemies.

One man was stung
two thousand times!
A big dog
was stung to death.

The assassin bug
is another killer.

This assassin bug
is creeping up
on a caterpillar.
Suddenly it plunges
its sharp beak
into the caterpillar's
furry body.
Then it squirts in poison.
The caterpillar's insides
turn to mush.

The assassin bug
sucks up the mush
and goes hunting
for another meal.

A female horsefly
punctures the skin
of horses and cows
with her
sharp mouth parts.
Then she sucks
their blood.

In Africa
some horseflies
even suck the blood
of crocodiles!

Some moths
are as big
as birds.

If a giant atlas moth
sat <u>right here</u>,
its wings would
cover both pages.

The atlas moth is huge,
but it still has enemies.
How does it
protect itself?
Its wing tips look
like snake heads.
Most animals are
afraid of snakes.
They leave the moth alone.

How far can you
stick out your tongue?

The long-tongued
sphinx moth
has a tongue
eleven inches long.
That's four times
as long as its body.

If a ten-year-old boy
had a tongue like that,
it would be as long as
his mother's car!

Look at these
huge cockroaches!
Luckily, you won't
find them
in your kitchen.

Madagascar hissing
cockroaches
live on an island
near Africa.

If a bird grabs one,
the cockroach hisses loudly.
Hssssssssssssssssss!
The startled bird
drops the cockroach
and flies away.

Some millipedes
ooze poison
when they are
frightened.

Indians in Mexico
used to grind up
millipedes
to make a deadly poison.
Before a battle,
they rubbed the poison
on their arrows.

Most bugs won't
hurt you.
Bugs are important.
They are food
for many other
creatures.
And they help trees
and flowers grow.

Bugs keep
our planet clean
by eating dead plants
and animals.

We couldn't live
without bugs—
even the biggest,
scariest
monster bugs!

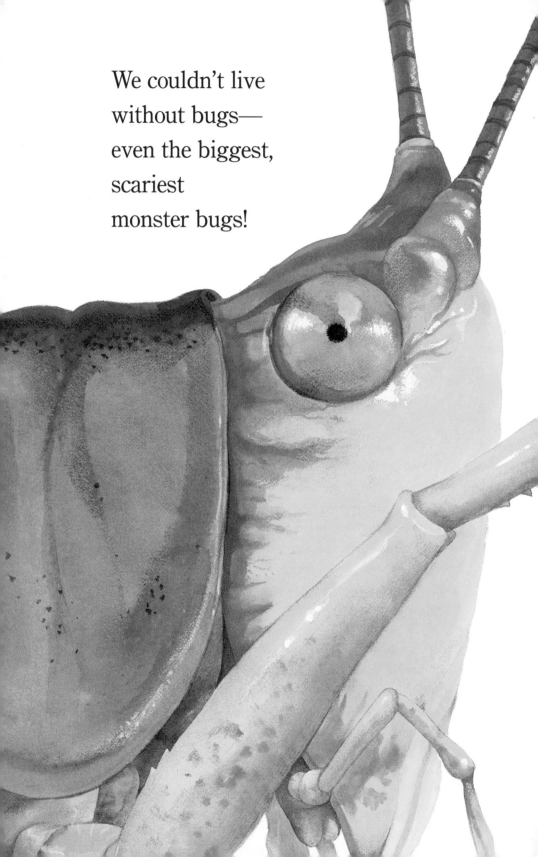